THE INUITS

SHIRLEE P. NEWMAN

THE INUITS

Franklin Watts   New York   Chicago   London   Sydney   A First Book

FOR HALEY AND TODD

Cover photograph copyright ©: Alaska State Museum
Map by Joe LeMonnier

Photographs copyright ©: Canadian Consulate: p. 3; Photo Researchers, Inc.: pp. 8 (Soames Summerhays), 15 top (George Holton), 19 bottom (Lowell Georgia), 35 top (Arthur Tress); Hudson's Bay Company Archives/Provincial Archives of Manitoba: pp. 12 top (Don Blair), 19 top, 21 bottom, 41 (both Richard Harrington), 33 (L.A. Learmonth); Wolfgang Kaehler: pp. 12 bottom, 13, 15 bottom, 23, 24, 30 bottom, 32, 50, 51, 53, 54; Rasmuson Library, University of Alaska, Fairbanks, Alaska and Polar Regions Department: pp. 17 top, 42 (both The William Van Valin Collection), 30 top; Anthro-Photo/Richard Condon: p. 17 bottom; The University Museum, University of Pennsylvania, (neg# S4-140729): p. 21 top; Alaska Division of Tourism: pp. 27, 35 bottom; The Bettmann Archive: pp. 37, 38; *Tundra Times*, Fairbanks, AK: p. 45; The Presbyterian Church (USA), Department of History, Sheldon Jackson Collection: p. 47.

Library of Congress Cataloging in Publication Data

Newman, Shirlee P.
The Inuits : by Shirlee P. Newman.
p. cm. — (A First book)
Includes bibliographical references and index.
Summary: Provides a look at the history, culture, and daily life of the Inuit people who live in the Arctic regions of the world, focusing on those living in North America.
ISBN 0-531-20073-6 (lib. bdg.)
1. Eskimos—Juvenile literature. [1. Eskimos. 2. Indians of North America.]
I. Title. II. Series.
E99E7N48 1993
973'.04971—dc20   93-18370   CIP   AC

CONTENTS

THE INUITS

PEOPLE OF THE NORTH

Inuits are native people who live in the Arctic, the northernmost parts of North America, Europe, and Asia. They are sometimes called Eskimos, an Indian word meaning "raw meat eaters." Those who live in North America and Greenland call themselves Inuits, which means The People. In other places, they may call themselves different names, which also mean The People. A 1977 meeting of people from all over the region decided that Inuit would be used for everyone, regardless of what they call themselves.

Inuits are people of medium height with black eyes, straight black hair, and high cheekbones. Some anthropologists think the Inuits first came to North America from Asia more than eight thousand years ago by paddling across the Bering Sea or walking across when it was covered by ice. Most of the people settled on the seacoast of what is Alaska today. Some

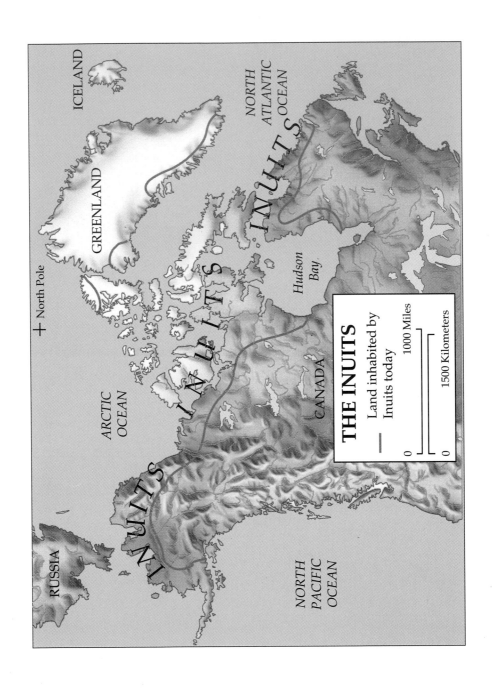

THE INUITS

— Land inhabited by
   Inuits today

0   1000 Miles

0   1500 Kilometers

ICELAND

GREENLAND

NORTH ATLANTIC OCEAN

INUITS

INUITS IN UITS INUITS

INNUITS

North Pole

ARCTIC OCEAN

Hudson Bay.

CANADA

RUSSIA

NORTH PACIFIC OCEAN

moved farther east and stayed around Hudson Bay in northern Canada. Others traveled farther south or on to Greenland. Those who settled in different regions adopted slightly different customs and spoke different dialects, but most could understand each other.

Winter is long and dark in the Arctic. Summer is short and full of light, for way up north the sun shines virtually day and night. The Arctic is often called "Land of the Midnight Sun." In past centuries, the Inuits had to cope with the varying length of seasons and availability of animals for food, clothing, and shelter. In some places, people moved to the coast in fall and lived upriver the rest of the year. In other places they moved upriver in fall and to the coast in spring and summer. Thus they hunted and fished where and when hunting and fishing were best.

Winter Homes ➤ Some people think all Inuits once lived in *igloos,* or houses made of snow. This isn't true. Igloo, or *iglu,* means any kind of house. Snowhouses were only built as all-winter homes in places where there was no stone or wood and snow was the only available building material. Central and northern Canada and the northern coast of Greenland are such places. In southern Alaska, winter homes were usually built of logs. In western Alaska, they were made of stone, sod (earth), or driftwood,

ABOVE, A HOUSE MADE
OF CARIBOU SKINS
STRETCHED OVER A
WOODEN FRAME. LEFT,
A TEMPORARY
DWELLING MADE OF
SOD AND ANIMAL SKINS
FOR A SUMMER
HUNTING CAMP

SUMMER TENTS ARE MADE OF SEAL SKINS STRETCHED OVER A FRAME AND ANCHORED TO THE GROUND BY STONES.

and were often built partly underground for strength and warmth. Sod covered a whalebone, wood, or stone frame. Most houses consisted of two rooms. The family lived, ate, and slept in one and used the other as a storeroom. Sod houses could usually be lived in for more than one winter.

Snowhouses ➜ Arctic hunters built snowhouses to protect themselves from cold and wind on hunting trips. These temporary dwellings could be built in an hour or two so hunters could stay overnight on the edge of *sea ice* while they hunted for seals or other sea animals. A snowhouse in which a family spent a whole winter took longer to construct as it had to be built more carefully. Two people usually worked together—one cuts blocks of packed snow while the other sets them together. Some snowhouses were round, others square or rectangular. Large snowblocks were placed in a spiral for the base of a round house. Smaller blocks were placed on top of the first row, still smaller blocks on top of the second row, and so on. All of the blocks tilted a little toward the inside for better support. Loose snow was pressed firmly into the cracks between them. A tunnel served as an entryway and kept out cold and wind. A block of ice or clear piece of sealskin was used as a window. Workers glazed inside walls with melting snow,

ABOVE, BUILDING A SOLID IGLOO REQUIRES THAT THE SNOW BLOCKS TILT INWARD FOR BETTER SUPPORT. RIGHT, A FINISHED IGLOO WITH THE LARGEST BLOCKS USED FOR THE BASE AND THE SMALLEST FOR THE TOP.

smoothing it onto walls and letting it freeze again. Sometimes built-up areas around the walls served as sitting and sleeping places. Other times a large snow platform with leather or furs was used for sitting, eating, and sleeping. The whole family usually slept close to each other.

Family Life in Winter ➤ In winter, men hunted for seal and walrus by waiting for the animals to come up to breathe through *aglus*, or holes in the ice. Some Inuit men also trapped foxes and other small animals, but for much of Inuit history women and boys did most of the trapping. Fathers spent stormy days making hunting equipment, tools, and the family's household utensils. Some men used a bow drill—a bow with a mouthpiece on one end of a crossbar and a sharp point on the other. He placed the mouthpiece in his mouth and held the point against whatever he was making. He moved the bow back and forth so the point acted as a drill.

Many fathers carved bone and wooden games for their children, dolls for their daughters, and animal figures for their sons. On warm days, he taught them how to fish through holes in the ice. Fathers taught boys how to hunt for seals at aglus, and, by the time a boy turned thirteen, he was expected to bring home his first seal.

RIGHT, THE INUIT BOW DRILL IS HELD IN MOUTH BY THE MOUTHPIECE ON TOP. THE BOW IS PULLED BACK AND FORTH MAKING THE DRILL REVOLVE TO BORE HOLES IN THE WOOD. BELOW, AN INUIT GIRL FISHES THROUGH THE ICE IN SPRING.

Mothers prepared and cooked the family's food over a *kudlik*, a lamp that was also used as a stove. The kudlik was an important item in an Inuit home, for it also provided light and heat and dried wet clothes. Fish oil, seal oil, or animal *blubber* was used for fuel. Wicks were made of moss or grass. To light the kudlik, a pointy stick was twirled against a notched piece of board until the powdered wood started to glow. Blowing on the glowing powder helped it become a flame that could be raised or lowered by moving the wick up and down. Inuits ate raw meat and fish when they were hunting or traveling, but it was usually boiled over the kudlik for the evening meal. Dried greens and seaweed collected in summer were often added to the cooking pot.

Sometimes the mother got the ingredients for her family's meals from the storeroom attached to the house. It might have contained meat, fish, and birds hunted during the summer. Frozen, dried, or salted, these preserved meats could be kept for months. Inuits ate almost every part of the animal, including the liver, heart, and intestines. *Muktuk*, a thin layer of fat under a whale's skin, was a favorite and considered a special treat.

Children → Babies spent their first year carried on a mother's back in her *amaut*, a hood on her jacket

ABOVE, YOUNG INUIT WOMAN WATCHING OVER HER KUDLIK TO MAKE CERTAIN THE FLAME DOESN'T GO OUT. LEFT, INUIT WOMAN SKINNING A SEAL. SHE MAY CHEW THE SKIN TO MAKE IT SOFT AND PLIABLE.

made for that purpose. They were cuddled and played with a great deal. When they grew too old to nurse, a seal's intestine was sometimes used as a baby bottle. Toddlers and young children played indoors most of the time in winter.

Nuglugaqtuq was a favorite winter game. A piece of bone with a hole in the middle was hung from the ceiling. Players tried to thrust a stick through the hole as the bone swung back and forth. The first one to put the stick through the hole was the winner. As children grew older, nuglugaqtuq was played with a series of holes and each hole counted for a different number of points. *Cat's cradle*, played with seal sinew as string, was a favorite game of adults as well as children. With practice, players became good at creating various figures such as animals by twisting the string around both hands.

In southwestern Alaska, many girls had a blunt "story knife" that their fathers carved for them of walrus tusk or driftwood. The girls drew pictures in the snow or dirt and made up stories about each other, animals, or everyday activities. The stories were simple when a girl was young and grew more complicated as she got older.

Both boys and girls often played the hopping game. Whoever could hop on one foot longest was the winner. In warm weather, an animal skin held by

LEFT, AN INUIT
MOTHER CARRIES
HER SLEEPING
BABY IN HER
AMAUT (HOOD).
BELOW,
ERKUAKTOK
SHOWS HOW
NUGLUGAGTUK
(CAT'S CRADLE)
IS PLAYED.

three or four people was used as a trampoline. Boys and girls learned to do tricks as they jumped up and down.

Neighboring families often took care of each other's children. Sometimes a family with many children gave one to a family with none. In bad times when there wasn't enough food some families felt it necessary to kill baby girls at birth rather than risk starving the entire family.

Community Life ➤ Groups of snowhouses were often built close together. Sometimes they were connected and had a common entrance so that two or three families could visit each other without going outside. A larger snowhouse served as a meeting place in some settlements. Ceremonies and celebrations took place there.

Although Inuits usually lived in small groups, they had no tribes or chiefs. Leaders were chosen for their special skills. On a hunting trip, the best hunter became leader. On a fishing expedition, the best fisherman gave orders but leaders often talked things over with others. Arguments might be settled by singing contests. If two men disagreed they made up songs that insulted each other and sang them at a community gathering. The man whose song was funniest, cleverest, or most insulting was the winner.

To survive in the Arctic, people had to share. Hunters gave food to widows, elderly people, or others who weren't able to hunt. It was considered good luck to share but if someone were considered lazy, hunters refused to share with him.

Clothing ➤ No one could live through icy Arctic winters without proper clothes. Two suits were necessary in winter. In summer, many days were still cool and a warm suit was worn for hunting, fishing, and *foraging* on the *tundra*.

AN INUIT CHILD
COMPLETELY
CLOTHED IN FUR
PLAYS IN THE SNOW.

LEFT, A POLAR BEAR SKIN STRETCHED OVER A RACK TO DRY IN THE SUN. BELOW, INUIT WOMAN WEARING COLORFUL TRADITIONAL CLOTHING IN ARVIAT IN CANADA'S NORTHWEST TERRITORIES.

It took days to prepare animal skins for clothes. Seal, caribou, fox furs, and bear skins were most often used. The skins were dried and cleaned with a bone scraper. Then they had to be twisted and softened, dampened, and stretched again. Sometimes skins were chewed to make them soft and pliable.

A family of four needed about twenty skins. A man's outfit took seven, a woman's outfit six, and each child needed three or four skins, depending on his or her size. Once the skins were prepared, women cut them with a curved knife called an *ulu*, and sewed them with bone needles and animal *sinew* as thread. Clothing styles varied in different regions, but men, women, and children dressed similarly. They wore a parka, or hooded jacket, trousers or leggings, long socks, boots, and mittens. In cold weather, the inner suit was worn with the fur next to the skin, and the outer suit was worn with fur on the outside. The air between the skins helped to keep in a person's own body heat. In warmer weather, only the inner suit was worn.

Shoes, called *kamiks* or *mukluks*, were made of caribou, reindeer, or sealskin. Canadian Inuits around Hudson Bay kept their feet warm and dry by wearing four different layers, an outside boot and three layers of socks, all made of animal skins. In some places footwear consisted of socks made of rabbit skin and an outer boot made of musk-ox, a shaggy, long-haired animal that looks like a buffalo. No matter what boots were made of, dried grass was spread between the layers as insulation. Women often chewed the skins before they were sewn into boots to make them soft and comfortable. They also chewed the family's kamiks each morning, for they usually stiffened overnight. Damp or wet clothes were beaten with a bone or stick and hung over the kudlik to dry.

Winter Transportation ➤ Inuits frequently had to travel long distances to find food. In winter, when waterways were clogged with ice, they walked or went by *komatik* (dogsled). The sled usually carried supplies, while people often walked or ran beside or behind it. Komatiks were made of wood, whalebone, or whatever solid material was available. Runners could be made of rolled-up sealskin or frozen fish. A sealskin was dampened, cut in half, and placed on the ground. The frozen fish was set along one side of each half. Then the sealskin was rolled up tightly with the fish inside and fastened with sinew. Runners were covered with soft mud and left out to freeze. Surfaces were smoothed down, and water was spread over them. The runners now had a hard, sliding surface that helped to keep the sled from getting stuck in soft snow.

INUIT MAN WITH HIS LEAD SLED DOG

A family usually had five or six dogs. These might be breeds called Siberian huskies, Alaskan malamutes, or Eskimo dogs, which could be a combination of breeds. They vary in size and weight, but all are especially adapted to the Arctic. Their tails curl above their backs to avoid being encrusted with snow. Adult dogs can sleep outside in the snow because they have thick outer fur and an inner coat of fine hair that keeps them from getting soaked. Puppies must be kept inside on cold nights. Eskimo dogs have heavy muzzles and strong legbones. They all have pointy ears that stand upright and oval-shaped faces. Instead of barking they often howl like wolves, from which they are descended. Sometimes their baying sounds like a chant.

The driver usually runs behind the sled. He might ride a bit every once in a while by standing on the back. When there's room his wife and/or children usually ride. Women and children often helped train dogs. Many women were as good at driving komatiks as men were. To start the dogs, the driver cracked his long whip and yelled "Mush!" The lead dog takes commands from the driver and turns, starts, and stops the other dogs. A team of five pulls a load of about 250 pounds (113 kg) and runs from 20 to 40 miles (32 to 64 km) a day. They run faster on empty stomachs so they're usually fed every other day. Some dogs help hunters track animals and dogs always share the meat. Most Arctic bays freeze over with thick ice. Gliding over smooth ice is easier than plowing through deep snow, so komatiks travel on ice whenever possible.

Spring and Summer ➡ Snow begins to melt by late spring. Summer's on the way. Families will soon move from winter homes into tents made of animal skins. The first time they see the sun, boys and girls run around shouting "Sekrenek nuiyok!" ("The sun has come up! He is back!") The sun may only be a dull, heatless ball now, but the children know it will bring warmth and light within a few weeks.

In places where water isn't still clogged with ice, whole communities may move to summer camps together. They traveled in *umiaks*, the same sort of boat used for hunting walruses and whales. The umiak was sometimes called the "woman's boat" because women usually paddled when it was used to carry families and their belongings. Men often traveled alongside umiaks or led the way in *kayaks*, which were also used for hunting on rivers, lakes, and streams. Although small and light, the kayak was even used for fishing and hunting at sea. The kayak's wooden or bone frame was completely covered with sealskin except for the opening where the paddler sat.

ABOVE, A TYPICAL INUIT
UMIAT USED FOR
HUNTING AND FAMILY
TRAVEL. LEFT, INUIT MAN
PADDLING A KAYAK.

To prepare the covering, hairs were scraped off the hides and skins were soaked in salt water for a few days. A short sealskin skirt drawn around the paddler's opening kept him and the kayak dry. A skillful paddler could roll completely over in the water without falling out. This maneuver came to be known as the "Eskimo Roll"; kayakers all over the world now practice it. The champion "Eskimo Roller" is mentioned in the *Guinness Book of Records*. Although the kayak was made for only one person, a hunter's wife and children sometimes went along with him, huddled together in the boat's dark, hollow inside.

The umiak's bone or wooden frame was also covered with animal skin, but the umiak's top was left open. Although it was lightweight and looked delicate, it could carry several families and their belongings and withstood rocks and ice better than some all-wood boats. At times a sealskin sail was used. Children constantly splashed the sail with water to keep it from drying out in the wind, and small pieces of sealskin were stowed in the boat to patch holes. Sometimes an umiak was loaded with a family's belongings and placed on a komatik and pulled by dogs until they reached open water. The sled and dogs were placed on the boat for the trip over water.

When they reached their camping site men and women set up tents together. Different groups

A TRADITIONAL INUIT SUMMER HUNTING CAMP

pitched differently shaped tents. Some were long and rectangular. Others were cone-shaped. For a cone-shaped tent, the size was marked by large stones placed in a circle on the ground. If wood was scarce, a single post was set up on a flat stone in the middle. Sealskin thongs were attached to the top of the pole and fastened to the stones at the base. Animal skins were stretched over the frame and held in place by the circle of stones. More stones were placed outside the tent to keep it from blowing down in a strong wind. The inside was usually divided into two sections. One was the sleeping area, the other was a kitchen and work area. An outdoor fireplace kept the inside free of smoke. When the tents were up, summer work began.

Fishing ➤ Men worked together to build dams to trap fish in shallow water as they came up the river or stream. Fish were then stabbed with spears or caught in nets or traps. Extra fish was dried in the sun and stored for winter in *caches*, pits dug in the ground and lined with stones. Sometimes caches were built like

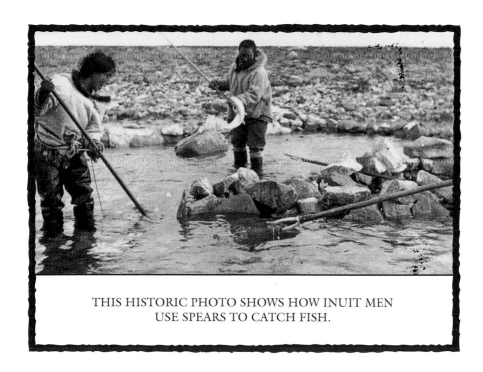

THIS HISTORIC PHOTO SHOWS HOW INUIT MEN
USE SPEARS TO CATCH FISH.

little huts up on stilts. Small animals would steal the fish if the caches were not constructed carefully. In a good summer, a family might fill four or five caches with 500 pounds (227 kg) of fish in each one. Women and children often fished alongside men.

Caribou Hunting ➤ Caribou belong to the reindeer family. They are a migratory animal. They move from place to place in search of food. Most caribou hunting was done in late summer or fall when the caribou moved north after feeding all summer farther south. Women and children sometimes chased the animals toward hunters who were hidden and armed with spears or bows and arrows. Other times caribou were driven into pits where they could be killed. They were also hunted in kayaks as they swam across lakes or rivers.

Foraging ➤ In summer, women and children gathered wild vegetables on the tundra. They also collected grasses to weave into baskets, for lamp wicks, and to insulate boots and sleeping platforms. Wild berries were used to make dyes. Seashells were collected along the shore to decorate their clothing.

ABOVE,
GRANDFATHER AND
GRANDSON PULL IN
THEIR FISHING NET
AT POINT HOPE,
ALASKA. RIGHT,
CARIBOU CROSSING
AN ICY RIVER.

INUITS AND EXPLORERS

In 1576, Martin Frobisher, an English explorer, set out to find a shortcut to Asia, as Christopher Columbus did in 1492. The shortcut Frobisher sought was called the Northwest Passage. He thought it went from the Atlantic Ocean to the Pacific through the Arctic Ocean and Bering Sea.

Frobisher landed on Baffin Island, now part of Canada, where he and his men met a group of Inuits. Some of them traded peacefully with the Englishmen, but others didn't get along. A fight broke out and Frobisher's men captured an Inuit and took him back to England. Frobisher later returned to the Arctic and captured three Inuits, a man, woman, and child, and took them back to England. This was not unusual. In those days explorers often brought back natives of different lands and showed them off like some kind of rare animal. The captured Inuits all died soon after landing in England.

MARTIN FROBISHER, AN ENGLISH EXPLORER, TRAVELED
TO THE ARCTIC IN SEARCH OF THE NORTHWEST PASSAGE.

LEFT, ROBERT E. PEARY ON THE DECK OF "THE ROOSEVELT," PEARY'S ICE-BREAKING SHIP NAMED FOR U.S. PRESIDENT THEODORE ROOSEVELT. BELOW, AT THE NORTH POLE. LEFT TO RIGHT: OOQUEH WITH NAVY LEAGUE FLAG, OOTAH WITH PEARY'S FRATERNITY FLAG, MATTHEW HENSON WITH AMERICAN FLAG, EGINGWAH WITH DAUGHTERS OF AMERICAN REVOLUTION PEACE FLAG, AND SEEGLOO WITH RED CROSS FLAG.

The search for the Northwest Passage continued for centuries and several other explorers met up with Inuits. Some of the meetings were friendly. Inuits traded kayaks, fresh meat, and fur clothing for knives, tools, and guns. Hundreds of ships were wrecked on ice, and many Europeans died of cold, disease, and starvation. Some Inuits taught friendly outsiders how to survive.

Admiral Robert E. Peary of the United States Navy was first to reach the North Pole, which was thought of as the "Top of the World." He planted the U.S. flag there on April 7, 1909. Peary had spent a whole winter studying Inuits. He had listened to their language, watched their habits, taken time to understand their ways. He won their confidence and friendship, and they taught him how to build snowhouses, construct caches, drive dog teams, and dress for the Arctic climate. Four Inuits were with him when he reached the Pole. Their names were Ootah, Seegloo, Egingwah, and Ooqueh. Peary said he never could have reached the Pole without their help.

INUITS AND FUR TRADERS

Furs were popular in the 1600s. Wealthy European and American men paid high prices for fur hats, collars for their overcoats, and scarves for their wives. British nobles and merchants and the Russian and Danish governments set up trading posts for the purpose of trading with Inuits for furs. Women had done most of the trapping before the *niovayit* (traders) came. Some Inuit men felt embarrassed to do "women's work," but the rifles, ammunition, and steel traps the niovayit offered them for furs meant they could hunt more efficiently. Niovayit also traded furs for matches, tea, coffee, sugar, and other things Inuits didn't have. Striking a match to light a lamp was faster than rubbing a stick against wood. A cup of tea or coffee warmed them on winter days. A lump of sugar tasted good as it melted in a child's mouth. Many Inuit men overcame their pride and became trappers.

[40]

Several different kinds of fur hung from trading post rafters. In Canada, there were muskrat, martin, mink, beaver, ermine, fox, otter, skunk, seal, lynx, wolf, and bear skins. In Greenland, caribou, reindeer, seal, fox, hare, and polar bear skins were piled onto sleds and hauled to the trading post. Beaver, fox, mink, muskrat, and seal were abundant in Alaska.

INUIT FUR TRAPPER TRADES ANIMAL SKINS FOR SUGAR, SALT, TEA, MATCHES, AND CHEWING GUM AT HUDSON'S BAY TRADING POST.

INUIT MEN HUNTING SEALS FROM KAYAKS
WITH HARPOONS

With new weapons and even greater demand for furs, many more animals were killed. In some places, caribou and seals became endangered.

Some Inuits worked for niovayit at other jobs. An Inuit named Otoochie (Little Seal Basking on Ice) managed a dog team and built sleds for traders who traveled long distances between trading posts on

Baffin Island. Pitsulak (Sea Pigeon) trapped, hunted, and carved figures of walrus ivory to be sent to Europe and sold there. Otoochie's wife made traders' winter clothing and did their laundry.

Traders and Inuits often learned each other's language and how to play each other's games. Checkers was popular with Inuits. Weather and radio stations were set up at remote posts. For the first time, Inuits could hear news of the outside world. Some posts became meeting places. Trappers and their families camped nearby when they came to trade and joined in social gatherings.

Some traders were fair with Inuits, while others didn't give them a fair deal. Russian traders treated them like slaves. They forced them to leave their homes and work wherever traders wanted. Thousands died of starvation, disease, and mistreatment. Russia sold Alaska to the United States in 1867, and an American company took over the Russian company. Trading companies gave Inuits credit for their furs. Inuits used the credit to purchase guns, matches, and other things. The American company insisted that Inuits pay up any debts at once. They gave Inuits only half credit for their furs and kept the other half to help pay their debts. Inuits were left without enough credit for supplies on which they had grown dependent.

INUITS AND WHALERS

Big whaling ships came to the Arctic from thousands of miles away in the 1800s. Electricity had not yet been invented, and whale oil was used to light and heat many American and European homes. *Baleen* (whalebone) was used to make women's corsets and hoops for the large hoopskirts they wore. *Ambergris* (a fluid from whales' intestines) was an ingredient in perfume that made the fragrance last longer.

Inuits had been paddling out to sea for hundreds of years trying to kill bowhead whales. A bowhead was larger and heavier than a bus. Inuits would risk their lives to kill one, for a single bowhead could supply a whole village with more fuel than a thousand seals. Ice blocked the ocean much of the time so they couldn't kill many.

INUITS PULL A HUGE BOWHEAD WHALE ONTO THE ICE
AT POINT HOPE, TIGARA, ALASKA.

Some Inuits worked for whalers or supplied them with fresh meat in exchange for ammunition, wood, tools, and foodstuffs such as potatoes and molasses. Whalers also gave Inuits liquor and taught them how to make it. Some whalers who spent the winter in the Arctic kidnapped Inuit women from Alaskan and Siberian villages. By the early 1900s, whalers had killed more bowheads with their modern equipment than Inuits had killed in all the years before whalers came. By 1912, bowheads were almost extinct.

INUITS AND MISSIONARIES

Inuits believed in *inuas*—spirits, or souls—and followed certain rules to please them. For instance, when Inuits died, they were not buried in the ground. They were dressed in their best clothes and left in a special place with some of their personal things. Inuits' spiritual beliefs also influenced how they hunted and killed animals. Fresh water was always poured over a seal's mouth when it was killed. Walrus and whale skulls were returned to the sea. Killing land and sea animals with the same weapons, or sewing land animal skins while hunting for sea animals were practices considered *taboo*, or forbidden. An *anakok*, or medicine man, was consulted when hunting was bad or an Inuit was sick. The anakok contacted the spirits to find out what could be done to improve hunting or cure the illness.

REVEREND JOHN KELLY, A PRESBYTERIAN MINISTER,
AND INUITS AT POINT BARROW, ALASKA

Missionaries of several different faiths came to the Arctic to convert Inuits to Christianity. The missionaries went from village to village and camp to camp and set up temporary churches in sod houses, snowhouses, and tents. They invited Inuits in for tea and told them about Jesus Christ.

Newcomers to the Arctic often brought diseases Inuits never had before and many got sick or died. Missionaries gave them medicine and advice on how to get well.

Missionaries helped make peace between Inuits and Indians. They set up schools and taught children to read and write in English, French, Danish, or Russian. Even though missionaries devised an Inuit alphabet, children weren't taught to read or write in Inuit. In some places, they weren't even allowed to speak their native language in school. Most Inuits eventually became Christians, but some older people still hold to traditional beliefs.

TODAY'S INUITS

Most Inuits now live in wooden houses in permanent villages. Some have no running water. A water truck comes around once each week and fills a barrel or tank in each house. Other Inuits live in apartment houses in Godthaab, Greenland, big cities in Alaska or Canada, and new towns in Siberia. Snowmobiles or all-weather vehicles pull sleds. Many Inuits no longer hunt and fish for all their food or make all their own clothes. They work at regular jobs and buy them at a store or order them from a mail-order catalog. Bringing things long distances by plane, truck, or boat is expensive, so they cost more in the Arctic than they do in other places. There aren't as many animals as there used to be, and there are limits on how many endangered animals can be hunted.

INUIT CHILDREN PLAYING HOCKEY IN THE SNOW AT
CAPE DORSET, IN CANADA'S NORTHWEST TERRITORIES

INUIT CHILDREN FROM GRISE FJORD,
ELLESMERE ISLAND, CANADA

Jobs are scarce in small villages. Many people leave home to work in lumber mills, mines, or fish-processing plants, but these jobs usually last only a few weeks. More and more young people move to larger towns or cities to find work. In recent years, the oil industry created many new jobs. At first white people were hired for the best ones. Now oil companies hire more Inuits and train them on the job. When oil drilling started on the Beaufort Sea, a technical school was set up in the tiny village of Tuktoyaktuk on Canada's Arctic coast. Inuits learned to use office machines and heavy equipment. Some graduates got good jobs but lost them when the oil company stopped drilling there.

Today's Inuits want to control their own lives. Thus, children are encouraged to study hard and go to college to become teachers, physicians, and lawyers. They are also urged to become business people, engineers, and government officials. More schools are being built, but some high school students still have to leave home and go to school far away. They live in dormitories and eat food they're not used to. They feel lonely without their parents and relatives. There are some Inuit teachers, but most are white and don't understand the Inuit language. In some places, students still aren't allowed to speak their own language in school.

INUIT GIRL AT A HUNTERS' FESTIVAL IN THE
MAGADAN REGION OF RUSSIA

INUIT WOMAN AT A HUNTERS' FESTIVAL IN THE
MAGADAN REGION OF RUSSIA

Although Inuits want their children to get ahead in the modern world, they want Inuit culture and tradition to survive. Older people come to school and teach children Inuit legends. They show them how to do beadwork, sew animal skins, make fishing traps. Local men take older boys out "onto the land" and teach them how to hunt seal by finding their aglus. They show them how to survive in storms and how to tell when ice is clean to melt and drink. In some places the school year is planned so children can hunt and fish with their parents.

In the 1980s, Canada's Northwest Territories began to include the Inuit language in important meetings and documents. Some places are now called by their original Inuit names instead of their English ones. Frobisher Bay is once again called Iqaluit, meaning fish camp. The Canadian government has helped Inuit artists, and their work is sold in galleries and museums in many parts of the world. Thomassie Qumak de Povungnituk has written an Inuit encyclopedia and dictionary that has helped spread Inuit culture. The Inuit Broadcasting Corporation presents programs in the Inuit language on television. Inuits from all over the Arctic come together each year for the Northern Games. They compete in Inuit sports, fish cutting, seal skinning, traditional dance, and *throat singing*.

Today's Inuits struggle between their need to make a living and their love of their land. They are now being paid for their lands and the oil that is pumped from them and sent to the rest of the world. Still, the Inuits worry about what's happening to their environment. Noise from offshore drilling has frightened away some bowhead whales. An oil spill in Alaska's Prince William Sound killed a great deal of wildlife. Some politicians want to explore wilderness areas for more oil, gas, and other natural resources. A pipeline to bring water from Alaska's rivers to California and a railroad across the tundra have been suggested. The land is our life, Inuits say. They don't want it spoiled.

The Canadian government and Inuit leaders recently reached an agreement that would create a new territory stretching from the border of the province of Manitoba to the North Pole. The territory would be called Nunavut, meaning Land of the People. It would be owned and governed by the seventeen thousand Inuits who live there.

GLOSSARY

Aglus   Breathing holes in ice.

Amaut   Hood for carrying a baby.

Ambergris   Fluid from a whale's intestine.

Angakok   Shaman, medicine man, or native doctor.

Baleen   Whalebone.

Blubber   Fat from whale or other sea mammal. The oil is extracted when the fat is melted.

Cache   Place for hiding or storing things.

Cat's cradle   A string game.

Foraging   Searching for food.

Igloo or *iglu*   A house, and especially a snowhouse.

Inuas   Spirits or souls.

Kamiks   Shoes made of animal skins.

Kayaks   Small pointed boats made of animal skins.

Komatik   Dogsled.

Kudlik   Lamp also used as stove and clothes dryer.

Mukluks   Shoes made of animal skins.

Muktuk   Thin layer of fat under a whale's skin.

Niovayit   Traders.

Nuglagaqtuq   A game.

Sea ice   Ice that forms on the ocean as a solid mass or ice flows.

Sinew   Animal tissue that connects muscle to bone.

Taboo   Forbidden.

Throat singing   Singing from deep in the throat. Sounds like the snap of tent rope in wind.

Tundra   Low-lying land between treeline and Arctic ice.

Ulu   Curved knife.

Umiaks   Boats made of animal skin. Comparatively large, always larger than kayaks.

FOR FURTHER READING

Angell, Pauline. *To the Top of the World*. Chicago: Rand McNally, 1964.

Avery, Susan and Linda Skinner. *Extraordinary American Indians*. Chicago: Childrens Press, 1992.

Cheney, Theodore A. Rees. *Living in Polar Regions*. New York: Franklin Watts, 1987.

Elliott, Paul. *Eskimos of the World*. New York: Julian Messner, 1976.

Jeness, Aylette. *Dwellers of the Tundra*. New York: Macmillan, 1970.

Meyer, Carolyn. *Eskimos: Growing Up in a Changing Culture*. New York: Atheneum, 1977.

Osborn, Kevin. *The People of the Arctic*. New York: Chelsea House, 1990.

Osinski, Alice. *The Eskimo: The Inuit and Yupik People*. Chicago: Childrens Press, 1985.

Smith, J.H. Grek. *Eskimos, the Inuit of the Arctic*. Vero Beach, Florida: Rourke, 1987.

Yue, Charlotte and David. *The Igloo*. Boston: Houghton Mifflin, 1988.

INDEX

ABOUT THE AUTHOR

The Inuits is Shirlee P. Newman's fourteenth book for children. Her books include biographies, fiction, folk tales, and a picture book, and she has worked as an Associate Editor on *Child Life Magazine*. She has published articles and stories in several other magazines and lives in Massachusetts.